A to Z Ice Cream Making Ice Cream at Home

For Total Beginners

by Lisa Bond

Table of Contents

Copyright © 2016 by sbBooks....5
Introduction....9
The History of Ice Cream....11
Method To The Madness....15
  Food Processor....16
  The Bag Method....16
  Freeze & Stir....17
Food Processor Ice Cream....18
  Simple Recipes....18
    Banana Ice Cream....18
    Vanilla Ice Cream....20
    Chocolate Ice Cream....21
    Peanut Butter Ice Cream....22
    Mint Chocolate Chip Ice Cream....23
Deluxe Recipes....24
  Orange Granita....24
  Frozen Fruit Yogurt....25
  Coconut Chai Banana Ice Cream....25
  Butter Maple Pecan Ice Cream....26
  Cheddar Ice Cream....27
  Grape Sorbet....28
Bag Method Ice Cream....29
  Recipes....31
    Simple Vanilla Ice Cream....31
    Raspberry Ice Cream....32
    Chocolate Ice Cream....32
    Strawberry Ice Cream....32
    Mint Choc Oreo Ice Cream....33
    Dairy Free Ice Cream....33
    Cinnamon Coconut Ice Cream....34
    Cherry Chocolate Chip....35
    Berry Ice Cream....35
    Coconut Cacao Ice Cream....35
Freeze & Stir Ice Cream....37
  Recipes....38
    Classic Vanilla....38

Chocolate Ice Cream....38
Strawberry Ice Cream....39
Honey-Peanut Butter Ice Cream....40
Matcha Ice Cream....41
Custard Ice Cream....42
Ice Cream Maker Ice Cream....44
Recipes....45
Easy Vanilla Ice Cream....45
Vanilla Ice Cream....46
Simple Chocolate Ice Cream....48
Cherry Cheesecake Frozen Yogurt....48
Peach Ice Cream....49
Rocky Road Ice Cream....50
Peanut Butter Ice Cream Deluxe....51
Extremely Chocolatey Chocolate Ice Cream....52
Zingy Lemon Ice Cream....53
Ice Cream Making Tips....54
Conclusion....56

Bill the Geek
bill@billthegeek.com

A TO Z
ICE CREAM
MAKING ICE CREAM
AT HOME
FOR TOTAL BEGINNERS
BY LISA BOND

Introduction

Welcome to this book. The following words are not to be taken lightly. They were not written lightly, but they are words of great importance. They are words which I have never used about any other topic. Until now! Are you ready? Here they are:

This book will change your life.

There, I said it and you know what? I mean it. This book is about making your own ice cream. That short description alone tells you everything you need to know about the importance of this book. Will this book actually change your life? Yes, yes it will. This book will tell you a little about ice cream and a lot about how to make it.

Once you are able to make your own ice cream, the possibilities are endless. You will have an infinite supply of the world's best treat. You will suddenly find yourself the talk of the town, the envy of your neighbors, the "Ice Cream Maker'.

With great power comes great responsibility. This book will empower you in your dessert creating skills. You should not take your new role lightly. Your family and friends will be asking you, nay begging you, to make more and more ice cream and do you know what? When you are able to make ice cream, it is your responsibility to make it for all those who want it.

If the previous paragraph scares you, then it has done its job. If you are not ready for this life challenge, then close this book and put it back on the shelf, preferably under another book. If you are reading this on an e-reader, then do not do that, just delete it. If you are not ready to become a cold-treat hero, then it is best to stop your journey now, wait for a while and try again when you are ready.

If this brief introduction has bolstered you, if it has ignited a fire in you, a fire which could melt a thousand ice cream scoops, then you are ready to begin your journey into the frozen wastelands of sugar and cream. You are ready to pick up the sprinkles and chocolate sauce and dive head first into the sundae of life.

It was at this point of the book that I was going to insert a little information about ice cream, a little "what is ice cream?' chapter, but you know what? If I need to explain what ice cream is to you, then you are not ready for this. Besides, who does not know what ice cream is? Instead, let's move onto the next chapter and find out a little about the history of ice cream.

The History of Ice Cream

If we do not know our history, then we are doomed to make the same mistakes. This sentiment is true for many things, and with ice cream too, I suppose. If we are going to dive in and create some of this sweet, sweet treat, then we should at least know a little about the background and where it came from. Was the ice cream of old like the ice cream of today? Was it made with "olde' ingredients? Was it literally just ice and cream? Let's find out.

The date is 500 BC, the location is Ancient Greece. Hippocrates, the father of modern medicine, is walking through the markets of Athens. He notices a vendor selling a sweet treat; snow mixed with honey and fruit. He pays for the delicious treat and eats it while continuing his stroll. One of his students approaches him after seeing Hippocrates buying the treat.

"Hippocrates, how is your treat?" asks the student.

"It is delicious," replies Hippocrates.

"I have been told that you recommend the very same dish for your patients," says the young student.

"I do indeed," says Hippocrates. "In fact, I believe it to liven the life-juices and increase the well-being of any patient." The young student nodded and smiled before going to purchase a treat for himself.

In 400 BC, the Persians froze rose water and vermicelli, in large ice houses, known as Yazds. They would mix the frozen rose water with saffron, fruits, and other complimentary flavors, serving it to the royalty of the day.

In 200 BC, the Chinese would fill various containers with flavored syrup, and cover the containers with snow and saltpetre, the salt acting as a catalyst for the freezing process.

The Roman Emperor Nero would send his men to gather ice from the mountains and would combine this ice with fruit to satisfy his sweet cravings. The Mughal emperors of India would have their horsemen ship the ice, at speed, from the colder parts of the country to be turned into sorbets.

The date is 1533 AD. The recipe for these dishes has not changed much. The Italian duchess, Catherine de' Merci has married the Duke of Orleans, later to become Henry II of France. She brings with her, her Italian chefs who have some outstanding recipes for flavored ices. Fast forward a hundred years. Charles I of England is impressed by the recipes which have been passed down through the generations. He does not want to share.

It is in the dark hallways, below the main floors of the grand palace, that he meets with the ice cream maker. The walls are hewn from great chunks of stone, cobwebs dance in the light breeze which comes from places it should not. The ghosts of a thousand ice cream makers wander the halls, looking for ice and fruit.

Charles sees the shadowy figure. He looks back, down the long tunnel, to make sure that he has not been followed. He approaches the hidden man and illuminates his hard features with the candle he is carrying, the royal ice cream maker blinks as his eyes adjust. Both men do not talk for an eternity before the silence is broken.

"Have you considered my offer?" asks Charles.

"I have," says the man.

"And?" asks Charles.

"I will accept," says the man.

"You will keep secret the flavors you make for the royal house?" asks Charles.

"I will." says the man.

"No one else will lay hands on your secret formulas?" asks Charles.

"They will not," says the man.

"Then a lifetime of wealth will be yours," says Charles.

No one is entirely sure if this story is true, the details have been hidden in mystery and folklore for centuries. No one is even sure if any of this took place, but if it did, then I am almost one hundred percent sure that it took place exactly like that.

The first published recipe for flavored ices appeared in 1674, in France. In England, ice cream recipes, ones containing real cream, began to pop up in the early 18th century. The Quakers brought their ice cream recipes to America with them, where the popularity of ice cream began to grow in the late 1700s.

The 19th century saw the change from expensive treat to inexpensive. Ice cream began to be made on a larger scale, with ice wells being used to freeze the treat, instead of ice houses. The 20th century saw freezers and ice cream blew up. Now everyone has access to the amazing dessert, the one Hippocrates attributed to a better life, the one royals would eat, the one which emperors sent men to the mountains for, the one which we all know and love, the one and only, ice cream.

Method To The Madness

I know, I know, you are sick of hearing of the humble beginnings of ice cream and want to get making some. Well, do not fear, for we are about to follow some recipes for great ice cream that you will be eating in no time.

Calm down! I can hear you shouting at me; you do not have an ice cream maker. Well, that is not a problem, as we are going to start with some simple recipes which do not require a machine at all. These methods range from minutes to hours, but one thing is for sure, all of them are delicious.

To make ice cream, you cannot simply mix cream with some sugar and flavoring and let it freeze, this sounds like the way ice cream is made, but it is not. To make ice cream, you need to churn the mix as it is freezing. Ice cream machines do this as they freeze the mixture. With other methods, there has to be some churning in the process.

When the ice cream mix is churned, smaller ice crystals are made, and more air is incorporated, this makes the ice cream fluffy and smooth. The finished product will have a foam-like texture and will be like eating frozen clouds (with chocolate chips and fudge inside them).

We are going to discuss three common non-machine methods, which involve some sort of churning. So what are the methods?

Food Processor

For this method, you need, of course, a food processor. The blade of a food processor will churn up the ingredients and incorporate the air into the mixture. When using this method, it is common to use frozen fruits, such as bananas, to allow the ice cream to be eaten immediately. The resulting ice cream can also be frozen once made.

The Bag Method

Using a bag also helps you to get at your ice cream immediately, and the workout for your arms will mean that you will have burned off the calories in the ice cream before you even eat it, maybe, I could be wrong on that one.

The bag method involves, first, mixing your ice cream mix with an electric mixer (or hand whisking it) before freezing it. The mixing gets the air into the mix so that the ice cream will be smooth and fluffy.

Once you have your mix mixed, you place it inside a resealable bag, or two to be safe, and squeeze out as much of the air as possible before sealing. You then place this mixture filled bag inside a bigger bag which is filled with crushed ice and salt (about 1 tablespoon of salt per cup of ice). The salt helps to lower the freezing point of the ice and creates a freezer like environment in the bag.

You then squeeze the air out of the ice filled bag and shake the bag vigorously. You can cover the bag with a towel if you like, to stop your hands from freezing. Shake the bag for 5-10 minutes, massaging the ice around the mixture as you are shaking it. The more vigorously you shake the bag, the smoother the ice cream will become.

Freeze & Stir

The last method to our madness is the freeze and stir method. Mix up your mixture as you would for the bag method, using an electric mixer or the power of your arms and a whisk. Once the mixture is whipped and creamy, pour it into a shallow dish and pop it in the freezer. After 45 minutes, bring the dish out and stir it with a spatula or spoon. Make sure to get in there and really mix it up.

Put the dish back in the freezer and remove it every 30 minutes to do the same as before; mix it vigorously and then pop it back in the freezer. After 2-3 hours, you should have some magnificent ice cream.

Now that you have seen some of the methods, our work here is done. Go on, get out of here and make some. Hold on, hold on, I am only joking. This book is far from over. Keep reading, for the next few chapters have some recipes which will delight and amaze.

Food Processor Ice Cream

Using a food processor is the easiest way to make ice cream and can be enjoyed immediately. Using this method is perfect for when you have an ice cream craving and want to be eating that ice cream in under two minutes. Making ice cream in a food processor usually uses fewer ingredients than traditional ice cream and takes advantage of either frozen fruit or ice to freeze the ingredients. Let's look at some easy to make recipes.

Simple Recipes

Banana Ice Cream

Ingredients: bananas

Method: This is the simplest ice cream you will ever make in your life. The only way you could have ice cream easier and quicker than this is if you had ice cream in your freezer already, and if you do, then why are you even making this. Go scoop some and eat it. Saying that, this recipe does require a little prep, so excuse me if this is your first time making this recipe.

The first step is to take some bananas; overripe bananas are perfect for this as you will not have the mushy texture once the ice cream is made. Peel the bananas, chop them into three of four pieces, place them in a sealable freezer bag, and place them in the freezer until frozen.

I like to freeze bananas as they ripen so that I have plenty frozen bananas for making this ice cream recipe and others. Step two is to take your frozen bananas and place them in your food processor. Place the lid on the food processor and process those frozen bananas. Once you have a creamy texture, you have your banana ice cream. Well done, you. If you would like the mixture to be more frozen and solid, you can place it in the freezer for half an hour, or you can make a big batch, eat some and freeze the rest.

You can make as much or as little of this as you like. As you are not adding any other flavors to the mix, you do not need to worry about the ratio of ingredients. Use as few or as many bananas as you like. Do not forget to top the ice cream with toppings of your choice. Peanut butter works well, as does chocolate sauce, though feel free to put on whatever you wish.

Vanilla Ice Cream

Ingredients: 2 Cups heavy cream, 2 cups whole milk, 3/4 cup sugar, 2 tsp vanilla, pinch salt.

Method: Take all of the ingredients and place them together in a large bowl. Which ingredients together until they are all combined and all of the sugar is dissolved. You can also mix the ingredients in your food processor if you want to incorporate a little air into the mixture. Once you have mixed all of the ingredients together, place the liquid in a sealable bag and put it in the freezer, taking care that does not spill, or the bag does not break.

Once your mixture has frozen, remove it from the freezer and break it into smaller pieces, pieces which will fit into your food processor. When you have all the pieces in your processor, blend them until smooth. Scoop the mixture into a dish and place back in the freezer until firm. Enjoy this take on the classic ice cream flavor.

Chocolate Ice Cream

Ingredients: 4 bananas, 1/4 cup cocoa powder

Optionalingredients: chocolate bar, honey, peanut butter, sea salt

Method: vanilla ice cream is great, but chocolate ice cream is where it is at (am I right?). This chocolate ice cream recipe is super simple but can become luxuriously exquisite with some optional additions.

The first step is to take some of your frozen banana from the freezer (I hope that you still have some in there, if not, then you can freeze some now and wait a little while). Place 4 bananas in your food processor and blend them until smooth. As you are doing this, combine the cocoa powder with a little hot water to form a thick paste (this will help the chocolate to be incorporated into the bananas). Add the chocolate paste to the smooth banana mix and process them together. Voila, you have chocolate ice cream.

This ice cream is naturally sweetened by the banana, but if it is not sweet enough for your taste, then you can add some honey (or other liquid sweeteners) and mix it in. How much you add is completely up to you. Another optional extra, to sweeten the ice cream, is a chocolate bar. Take a bar of your choice and cut it into small pieces (or process it into small pieces). Add these pieces to your ice cream to give it a "Ben & Jerry's' feel.

The icing on your cake is the last two optional extras. Take your ice cream and smother it in some peanut butter. Sprinkle some sea salt on top of the peanut butter and enjoy one of the greatest creations known to man (and of course, woman).

Peanut Butter Ice Cream

Ingredients: 3 bananas, 3 Tbsp peanut butter, optional sweetener

Method: You should know by now to have pieces of frozen banana on hand in your freezer. This recipe uses them too so make sure to freeze them now if you do not have any to hand. Once you have your frozen bananas, place three of them in your food processor with 3 tablespoons of peanut butter. Blend the ingredients until smooth.

You can add some sweetener if you wish, honey of maple syrup perhaps. You can also place the mix back in the freezer if you would like it a little more frozen.

Mint Chocolate Chip Ice Cream

Ingredients: 2 bananas, 1/8 tsp peppermint extract, chocolate chips

OptionalIngredients: green food coloring, spinach

Method: take the chocolate chips (you can also use carob chips or cocoa nibs) and blend them in your food processor until they become small chocolatey pieces. Set the chocolate pieces aside for later.

Take 2 frozen bananas from your freezer (I hope you have a good stock of them in your freezer) and place them in our food processor. Add the peppermint extract and blend them together. Once they are smooth, add the chocolate pieces and blend one more time to incorporate them.

This delicious recipe needs no additional toppings (though if you were to add some, no one would stop you). The finished product will not resemble the product you would find in the supermarket; it will not be green in color. If you would like to replicate the color, you could add a little green food coloring to your recipe, or some spinach for a nutrient boost.

Deluxe Recipes

Now that you have mastered some of the classic ice cream recipes, it is time to step it up a notch and create some ice cream flavors which will delight not only you but your friends and family too.

Orange Granita

Ingredients: 2 cups orange juice, 3 Tbsp maple syrup, 3 Tbsp sour cream, pinch salt

Optional ingredients: ground cardamom

Method: Take the orange juice, either freshly squeezed or store bought (no sugar added), and add the maple syrup. Once it is thoroughly mixed, place the mixture in a container and freeze it for two hours. Take the mixture out of the freezer and mix with a fork, every 30 minutes. Once the mixture is frozen in little ice pieces, take the sour cream and add the salt, and the cardamom if you are using it.

Take four small bowls or glasses and divide the sour cream mixture evenly between them. Top the sour cream mix with the granita (the frozen orange mix). Grab a spoon and enjoy this treat which is perfect for your deck on a hot summer's day.

Frozen Fruit Yogurt

Ingredients: 1 cup yogurt, 1/2 vanilla bean, 16oz frozen peaches, 1 Tbsp apple juice concentrate, 1/3 cup sugar.

Optional ingredients: any other frozen fruit

Method: put the yogurt, peaches, apple juice and sugar into your food processor. Take the half vanilla bean pod and slice it lengthways. Scrape the seeds from the bean and add these to the blender too. You can save the pod to flavor things if you wish, soak it in some liquid or place it in some sugar for the flavor to be absorbed.

Once you have all the ingredients in the food processor, blend them all together. Once the frozen treat is blended together, you can either serve it immediately, or you can place it back in the freezer to serve at another time. You can substitute the frozen peaches for any other frozen fruit, or combine fruits to create exciting flavors

Coconut Chai Banana Ice Cream

Ingredients: 3 frozen bananas, 5 Tbsp coconut cream/milk, 1/4 tsp cardamom powder, 1 tsp cinnamon, 2 tsp minced ginger, 1/2 vanilla bean pod

Method: add the bananas, coconut cream (or milk), cardamom powder, cinnamon and ginger to your food processor. Slice the vanilla pod lengthways and scrape out the seeds, placing them in the food processor too. Keep the vanilla pod to flavor things (see the previous recipe). Blend all of the ingredients until they are creamy and smooth. Serve the ice cream immediately or freeze it, if you would like to keep it for another time.

Butter Maple Pecan Ice Cream

Ingredients: 4 frozen bananas, 1/2 cup almond butter, 1/2 cup maple syrup, 1/4 cup tahini, 1tsp cinnamon, 2 tsp vanilla extract, 1 cup pecans

Method: Take the bananas, almond butter, maple syrup, tahini, cinnamon and vanilla, and add them all to your blender. Once they are all blended, stir in the pecans and enjoy (or freeze for later).

Toptips: you can substitute the almond butter for any other nut butter. If you are subbing for another nut butter, try to use unsweetened, or adjust the amount of maple syrup you add to the mixture. If you do not like pecans, then you can leave them out. You can also pre blend the pecans if you would like smaller pieces of nuts through your ice cream.

Cheddar Ice Cream

Now, before we go any further, I just want to assure you that this is not a joke. Yes, you are about to get a recipe for cheddar ice cream. Do not shrug your shoulders like that and do not turn up your nose. How about you try it before you judge it?

Ingredients: 2 cups milk, 1 Tbsp arrowroot, 1/2 cup sugar, 10oz cheddar cheese, 1/2 tsp vanilla extract, pinch salt, pinch pepper

Method: take the time to bring your ingredients to room temperature, by letting them sit in a room. You can chill out and watch Netflix while this is happening. This helps the cheese to become soft and easier to incorporate into your mixture.

Take the milk, arrowroot and sugar and whisk together in a saucepan. Place on a medium heat and bring to a simmer. When it is simmering, grate the cheese and add it into the mix. Whisk constantly until the mixture comes to a boil. Turn off the heat and remove the saucepan from the stove. Continue to whisk the mixture and add in the vanilla, salt and pepper.

Let the mixture cool before putting it in a sealable bag and placing that bag in the freezer. When the mix has frozen, break it into smaller chunks and blend it in your food processor. Once it is smooth and creamy, put it back in the freezer for another thirty minutes.

Serve to your guests and watch them be amazed at how clever you are!

Grape Sorbet

Ingredients: 3 cups frozen green grapes, 4 mint leaves, 3 Tbsp maple syrup, 2 tsp lemon juice, pinch salt

Method: Place all of the ingredients in your food processor and blend until smooth. Once the mixture is smooth, transfer it to a container and place that container in the freezer for another two hours. Enjoy this zesty creation on your patio on a warm spring evening.

With a simple food processor, you can make a plethora of ice cream flavors, from simple vanilla to weirdly satisfying cheddar cheese. Most of the recipes can be made in minutes (if you have planned ahead) and can be enjoyed straight away. All of the recipes are delicious and the great thing about making ice cream this way is that you can really play around with the recipes and invent your own flavors and customizations. If you have a food processor, then go plug it in and make some ice cream. If you do not have a food processor, then read on for some more methods and recipes.

Bag Method Ice Cream

This method of making ice cream requires a lot of elbow grease. It is the most labour intensive method and will require you to shake a bag vigorously for five to ten minutes. Here are some things you may wish to have before you start the recipes:

•Lots of ice in your freezer

•Salt (kosher salt works best)

•Pint sized Ziploc bags, for the ice cream mix

•Gallon sized Ziploc bags, for the ice and salt mix

•Towel, to wrap the bags in and stop your hands from getting too cold

All of the recipes in this chapter are going to involve mixing the ingredients, placing them in the smaller bag, and shaking the ice cream inside the bigger bag, filled with ice and salt. Each recipe is going to use the same method, so when we say to "shake the mix', here is what we mean:

•Place the mixed ingredients in the pint sized bag

•Remove as much air from the bag as you can and seal

•Fill the gallon sized bag half full with ice

•Add 1/2 cup of salt to the ice

•Mix the salt and the ice together

•Place the small bag (the one with the ice cream mixture) inside the larger bag

•Remove as much air from the large bag as you can

•Seal the large bag

•Cover the bags with a towel if you wish (or use oven gloves too)

•Shake the large bag for 5-7 minutes

•Open both bags carefully and check the ice cream

•If it is soft and ice cream like, eat it

•If you want it firmer, seal the bags and shake some more

•If the ice has melted, add some more

The advantage of this method over the food processor method is that it allows you to use more milk based recipes and freeze the mixture which incorporating air into it. This method does not rely on frozen fruit to provide the cold, instead, the combination of ice and salt makes the mixture inside freeze quickly, while the shaking adds the air.

This method can also be a little messy, especially if one of your bags has a hole in it. You can shake the bags outside, or do it over a sink to avoid having to do any clean up after your ice cream is made.

Recipes

Simple Vanilla Ice Cream

Ingredients: 1/2 cup half-and-half, 1 Tbsp sugar, 1 tsp vanilla extract

Method: combine the three ingredients and add to the smaller bag. Shake the mix and enjoy some simple vanilla ice cream with the hot pie of your choice.

More Vanilla Ice Cream

Ingredients: 1/2 cup milk, 1/2 cup heavy cream, 1/4 cup sugar, 1/4 tsp vanilla extract

Method: combine all of the ingredients and place in the small bag. Shake the mix and enjoy. Test taste this against the previous vanilla recipe to find out which one you like the best.

Raspberry Ice Cream

Ingredients: 1 cup half-and-half, 1/2 cup raspberries, 1/4 cup sugar, 2 Tbsp evaporated milk, 1 tsp vanilla extract

Method: combine all of the ingredients in the small bag and place inside the larger bag. Shake the mix and check on it every so often. Kids will love this recipe, with little dots of red raspberry mixed into the ice cream.

Chocolate Ice Cream

Ingredients: 1/2 cup milk, 1 Tbsp sugar, 1/4 tsp vanilla extract, 1 tsp chocolate syrup

Method: mix all of the ingredients together and place in the smaller bag. Place in the larger bag and shake the mix. This recipe will make approximately one serving of ice cream, but you can adjust the recipe to make more by doubling or tripling the ingredients. You can use chocolate milk if you want, but be sure to add a little more sugar to the recipe.

Strawberry Ice Cream

Ingredients: 1/2 cup heavy cream, 1/2 cup milk, 1/2 tsp vanilla, 3 Tbsp pureed strawberry, 3 Tbsp sugar

Method: Mix all of the ingredients together and place in the small bag. Shake the mix and either enjoy immediately or freeze for later. Add some slices of strawberry to your bowl of ice cream for a little upgrade to your ice cream.

Mint Choc Oreo Ice Cream

Now we are talking; this is my kind of ice cream.

Ingredients: 1 cup whipping cream, 2 Tbsp sugar, 1/4 tsp peppermint extract, 4 drops green food coloring (optional), 5 Oreos

Method: mix the whipping cream, sugar and peppermint and add to the smaller bag. You can add the food coloring to the mix if you want the green tint reminiscent of the store bought ice cream. Shake the mix and then transfer to a bowl. Crush the Oreos and stir them into the ice cream. Enjoy now or transfer to the freezer for later (who are we kidding? Of course we are eating it now).

Dairy Free Ice Cream

All of the recipes on this list, so far, contain dairy. It is easy to make dairy free ice cream if you substitute some of the ingredients. Here is an entirely dairy free recipe for you to try.

Ingredients: 1 cup soy milk, 2 Tbsp sugar, 1 tsp vanilla extract

Method: mix all of the ingredients and add to the smaller bag. Shake the mix and get ready to enjoy some dairy free ice cream that you just made in your own kitchen, from three ingredients, and in under fifteen minutes.

Cinnamon Coconut Ice Cream

Ingredients: 2 cans coconut milk, 1/4 cup honey, 3 egg yolks, 2 tsp cinnamon

Method: Now we are getting into some high-class ice cream with egg yolks. Separate 3 eggs and use the yolks for the ice cream. You can use the whites to make a low-fat omelette for your breakfast. Add the honey and cinnamon to the egg yolks and whisk together. Add the coconut milk (at room temperature if possible), and whisk together.

Put the mixture into the smaller bag (or half if it will not all fit). Shake the mix and enjoy immediately or freeze for later. This is the kind of ice cream which will dazzle and amaze any of your friends and family.

Cherry Chocolate Chip

Ingredients: 1 cup milk, 3 Tbsp sugar, 3 drops almond extract, 2 Tbsp chocolate chips

Method: Mix the milk, sugar, almond extract and chocolate chips and add to the small bag. Shake the mix and enjoy some berry chocolate chip ice cream (the almost extract gives the ice cream a berry flavor).

Berry Ice Cream

Ingredients: 1 cup half-and-half, 1/3 cup powdered sugar, 1/4 cup frozen berries

Method: mix the half-and-half and powdered sugar together until the powdered sugar is dissolved. Add the berries to the mix and place in the smaller bag. Shake the mix and at your ice cream while imagining you are on a Mediterranean patio with the sun bouncing off the ocean.

Coconut Cacao Ice Cream

Ingredients: 1 1/2 cups coconut milk, 1/2 cup heavy cream, 1/2 tsp vanilla, 2 Tbsp sugar, pinch salt, coconut flakes, cacao nibs

Method: combine the milk, cream, vanilla, sugar and salt. Whisk these ingredients together. Once incorporated, add the coconut flakes and cacao nibs (as much of each as you want) to the mix and place in the small bag. Shake the mix and taste what dreams are made of.

It is so simple to make your own dairy, and dairy-free, ice cream in under 15 minutes. You will get a sense of satisfaction from shaking up the ice cream to mix it, incorporate air, and freeze it. The satisfaction you get will make the ice cream taste even better. You can play about with the recipes, substituting the ingredients and altering the amounts to get the taste you want.

Pro tip: to add some fun to your ice cream making experience, use snow instead of ice. You should still add the salt to expedite the freezing process. Kids and adults alike will be delighted at the notion of making ice cream with snow (even if you do not eat the snow). There is something magical about this.

Pro tip 2: make this a family (or group) exercise to alleviate the burn in your arms from shaking the ice cream for up to ten minutes. Have one person start and pass it on when they can no longer shake it. Have a dance party where you dance around shaking the bags, passing it from person to person as you rock out to your favorite Queen or Justin Bieber song*.

*Queen is the recommended music for great ice cream. Bieber will work, but it does not taste as creamy (seriously! Why would I lie to you about this?).

Making ice cream in a bag is fun, but there are times when you want to give your arms a rest and still make great ice cream. What if your arms are cramping from so much ice cream making and you do not have a food processor, is there a third method you can use? (hint: we already established that there were three methods). Read on to find out (even though you already know the answer).

Freeze & Stir Ice Cream

The freeze and stir method is not as labour intensive as the bag method but still allows you to make great dairy ice cream. The one thing you do need for this method is time. The actual making of the ice cream does not take a lot of time, but you do need to stir the ice cream occasionally as it freezes. Make this ice cream when you are doing something around the house and set an alarm to remind you to stir the ice cream so that it turns out creamy and delicious.

When you are stirring the ice cream, you will need to stir it vigorously, enough to mix the ingredients together and incorporate some air, but you do not need to be as vigorous as the bag method. Well, enough talking about this method, let's start making some ice cream.

Recipes

Classic Vanilla

Ingredients: 4 cups half-and-half, 1/2 cup heavy cream, 3/4 cups sugar, 2 tsp vanilla extract, pinch salt

Method: whisk the half-and-half, cream, sugar, vanilla extract and salt together until all the ingredients are mixed, and some air has been incorporated into the mix. Pour the mix into a shallow pan and place the pan in the freezer. After 30 minutes, open the freezer and stir the mixture vigorously with a spatula or spoon. Place the pan back in the freezer. Continue to do this every 30 minutes for the next three hours and your ice cream should be ready to eat.

Chocolate Ice Cream

Ingredients: 14oz can sweetened condensed milk, 2 cups heavy cream, 1/2 cup cocoa powder, tsp vanilla extract, pinch salt

Method: whisk together the milk, cocoa powder, vanilla and salt until they are all combined. In a different bowl whisk the cream. You can do this by hand, or you can use an electric mixer. A mixer on medium speed will have firm peaks appearing in around two minutes.

Fold one cup of the whipped cream into the first mixture until it is completely combined. Pour this mix back into the rest of the whipped cream and fold until it is all mixed together. Pour this mix into a shallow pan (or loaf pan) and put it in the freezer. You do not need to mix this mixture every 30 minutes, instead leave it in the freezer for two to three hours. When it is frozen, scoop it into bowls and enjoy.

Strawberry Ice Cream

Ingredients: 1 pound frozen strawberries, 2 cups heavy cream, 14oz sweetened condensed milk, tsp vanilla extract, pinch salt

Method: allow the strawberries to rise in temperature slightly by taking them out of the freezer ten minutes before starting this recipe. Use a blender/food processor to cut the strawberries into small chunks. You can also do this by hand with a knife (though it will take a little longer).

Mix the milk, vanilla, salt and strawberry chunks together in a bowl. In a separate bowl, whisk up the cream, either by hand or with an electric mixer until firm peaks form. Fold a cup of the cream into the strawberry mixture and then pour this mixture back into the whipped cream. Blend the mixtures together until thoroughly mixed.

Pour the mixture into a shallow pan, or loaf tin, and place it in the freezer. Let it sit in the freezer for 4-5 hours before scooping into bowls and enjoying with friends around the fire.

Honey-Peanut Butter Ice Cream

Ingredients: 1/3 cup smooth peanut butter, 3 Tbsp honey, 14oz sweetened condensed milk, 1/4 tsp crushed red pepper flakes, 1/4 tsp cayenne, pinch salt, 1 cup heavy cream, 4 peanut butter cookies, 1 cup peanut brittle

Method: this ice cream recipe is delightfully delicious. Do not worry about the calories, I mean, sure there are lots of them but do not worry about them, instead think of kittens, falling off tables.

Mix the peanut butter and honey together (runny honey works best here). In a separate bowl, mix the condensed milk, red pepper flakes, cayenne and salt. When they are all combined, set the bowl aside. In another bowl, whip up the cream until firm peaks form. Use an electric mixer if you are feeling especially lazy.

Fold half of the whipped cream into the milk mixture and then fold the other half until it is thoroughly mixed. Pour half of the mixture into a shallow dish and dollop the peanut butter and honey mix on top. Crush the peanut butter cookies and sprinkle them on top too. Pour the rest of the mixture on top and freeze for at least three hours.

When you are ready to serve it, scoop into bowls and sprinkle some crushed peanut brittle on top. You can garnish this with honey too if you wish to add some silky smooth sweetness.

Matcha Ice Cream

Ingredients: 14oz sweetened condensed milk, 2 tsp match powder, 1 tsp vanilla extract, pinch salt, 1 cup heavy cream

Method: this ice cream recipe is extremely simple, but after tasting your taste buds will be so delighted that it will feel as if fireworks are exploding in your mouth.

Whisk the condensed milk, matcha powder, vanilla and salt together until mixed. In a separate bowl, whisk up the cream, either by hand or with an electric mixer. Once stiff peaks form on the whipped cream, spoon half of it into the condensed milk mixture and fold in until incorporated. Fold in the other half and then freeze in a shallow pan for 3 hours.

Custard Ice Cream

Ingredients: 2 1/4 cups heavy cream, 1 cup milk, pinch salt, 4 egg yolks, 1/2 cup maple syrup

Optional ingredients (1): 1 cup raisins, 1/4 cup rum

Optional ingredients (2): your choice of berries

Method: okay, I have gone easy on you so far with this ice cream making business. Now we step it up a notch. In a saucepan, heat the cream, milk and salt on a medium heat until they begin to simmer. Whisk the egg yolks together in a bowl and when the mixture on the stove begins to simmer, pour the hot mixture slowly into the yolks. Stir constantly as you add the mixture, little-by-little. When you have mixed this all together, put the saucepan back on the stove and slowly pour the mixture back into the pan, again stirring constantly as you do this.

Turn the heat down to medium-low and stir the mixture for 4 minutes, or until the mixture begins to thicken. When it does thicken, remove it from the heat and add the maple syrup. Allow this mixture to cool completely. Pour the cooled mixture into a baking dish and put it in the freezer.

After 45 minutes, remove the mixture and stir it vigorously with a spatula. Put it back in the freezer for 3-4 hours, stirring it vigorously every 30 minutes. When it is frozen, enjoy some of the best ice cream you have ever tasted.

Variation one: when you are waiting for your mix on the stove to begin to simmer, combine the raisins and rum in a bowl to allow the raisins to soak up the rum. Put the rum raisins in the fridge. When you remove the custard mix from the heat and add the maple syrup, add three tablespoons of the rum from the raisin bowl too. Fifteen minutes before serving your ice cream, remove it from the freezer and when it has softened slightly, add the rum soaked raisins and stir them in. You just made rum raisin ice cream.

Variation two: make the custard ice cream and fifteen minutes before freezing, remove it from the freezer to soften. When it has softened slightly, stir in some berries of your choice. Delicious!

Freezing and stirring is a great way to make ice cream. It is easy, cheap and makes delicious treats for you and all of your friends. We have looked at three inexpensive ways you can make ice cream, all with equipment you probably have lying around your house. If you really want to go all out and make some great ice cream, you just have to suck it up and take the plunge.

Ice Cream Maker Ice Cream

You want to make some ice cream. You do not have a food processor. You do not want to shake a bag for ten minutes. You do not want to have to take your ice cream out of the freezer to stir every thirty minutes. You have a few bucks to spare. You have decided that you are ready. You are buying an ice cream maker. What do you need to know?

•There are many machines on the market. A higher price usually means a larger quantity of ice cream or a better quality of machine, but not always.

•If you do not want to make ice cream by hand, then you should not go for a hand cranked model. Invest in electric.

•The freshest ingredients give the best quality ice cream. Good ingredients make good ice cream.

•Most good machines will create ice cream in 30 minutes (this does not include your prep time).

•Compressor models make the best ice cream, but can be more expensive and make less quantity than some other machines.

•Smaller models are usually louder.

•Ice cream recipes can be used with any machine. Refer to your user manual for how to use them.

•Your ice cream maker may need you to freeze the bowl for 12-24 hours before adding the mix. Refer to your user manual.

•Most ice cream makers will make soft scoop ice cream, but putting your ice cream in the freezer for a few hours will make it more solid.

•Home made ice cream will be cheaper than premium ice cream bought from the store, but not cheaper than the lower end ice cream. It will, however, have better ingredients.

Recipes

Easy Vanilla Ice Cream

Ingredients: 2 quarts half-and-half, 1/2 pint heavy cream, 1 1/2 cups sugar, 4 tsp vanilla extract, pinch salt

Method: mix all of the ingredients in a bowl until they are all incorporated and then follow the instructions of your ice cream maker. There you go, your first ice cream maker recipe is as simple as that!

Vanilla Ice Cream

Ingredients: 1 cup heavy cream, 1 cup full-fat milk, 1 1/2 cup sugar, 1 vanilla pod, 3 large egg yolks

Method: pour the cream and milk into a saucepan. Add half of the sugar. Cut the vanilla pod lengthways and scoop out the seeds. Put the seeds in the pan with the mix too. Cut the vanilla pod into three of four pieces and add this to the mix also.

Heat the mixture over a low heat, making sure to mix constantly with a spoon, until the mixture begins to boil. Take the saucepan off the stove and let to sit somewhere for thirty minutes, giving time for all of the flavor of the vanilla pod to be absorbed. I bet you want to go back to the easy vanilla ice cream recipe, don't you?

Put the egg yolks, and the remainder of the sugar, in a bowl together. Use an electric mixer (or hand whisk if you are feeling energetic) until the eggs and sugar combine and thicken. They should be paler in color and fall from your beater in thick strands.

Scoop out some of your boiled milk/cream mix and add it to your egg/sugar mix. Beat the two together to create a thinner mixture (do not add too much). Reheat the rest of the milk/cream mixture, stirring constantly, until it comes back to a boil. When it does, take it off the heat and slowly stir the egg mixture into it.

Return the pan to a low heat (you can give up and go back to the easy vanilla ice cream mix if you want to) and cook it for a further eight minutes, stirring constantly. The mixture should not boil. You should be checking it as it runs off the back of your spoon. If it is thick enough to coat the back of your spoon, then your custard mix is ready.

As you are cooking for the eight minutes, grab a large bowl and fill a third of it with iced water. Place a smaller bowl inside this. The smaller bowl should be big enough to hold the custard mix as this is where you will be pouring it now. Let it cool in this bowl for twenty minutes, stirring occasionally so that a skin does not form on the top of your custard.

Now put your mix in the fridge for at least three hours (overnight is preferable). Once your mixture is chilled sufficiently, use your ice cream maker as per the instructions. This method takes some time, but it really is worth it. The recipe can seem daunting, and there is a chance of it going wrong and the eggs curdling. Take the time to get to know the recipe and have everything ready before you start to make the ice cream.

Good luck!

Simple Chocolate Ice Cream

Ingredients: 14oz sweetened condensed milk, 2 cups heavy cream, 2/3 cup chocolate syrup

Method: Mix the condensed milk and chocolate syrup together. In a separate bowl, whip the heavy cream until firm peaks form. Fold the two mixtures together and pour into your ice cream maker. Use the ice cream maker as per the manufacturer's instructions. Super easy and super yummy.

Cherry Cheesecake Frozen Yogurt

Ingredients: 8oz cream cheese, 1 cup sugar, 1 Tbsp lemon juice, 3 cups Greek yogurt, 2 cups fresh cherries

Method: before making your ice cream, make sure that your cherries are pitted and chopped (unless you like cherry pits in your ice cream). Allow the cream cheese to sit out of the fridge for a while so that it softens. When the cream cheese is soft, mix it with the sugar until they are combined. Stir in the lemon juice and then begin to add the yogurt, one cup at a time, stirring each cup of yogurt until it is thoroughly combined. Your mixture should be smooth and creamy.

Stir in your cherry pieces and then use your ice cream maker as it was intended to be used by the people who made it. A simple recipe, with simple ingredients, which will give you a complex and delicious, low-fat, frozen yogurt treat.

Peach Ice Cream

Ingredients: 2 1/2 pounds fresh peaches, 1/2 cup sugar, 1 pint half-and-half, 14oz sweetened condensed milk, 12oz evaporated milk, 1 tsp vanilla extract, 2 cups whole milk.

Method: before starting to make the ice cream, peel, pit and chop your peaches. Cut the pieces pretty small, and you can chill or freeze them before adding if you like. Once you are happy to use your peaches, blend them with the sugar and half-and-half until you have a peach puree.

Mix the peach puree with the condensed milk, evaporated milk, whole milk and vanilla. Mix until all of the ingredients have been incorporated and then use your ice cream maker for its true purpose: to make ice cream.

Enjoy this ice cream with a slice of hot peach pie, or on its own as a late night snack that you don't tell anyone about.

Rocky Road Ice Cream

Ingredients: 14oz sweetened condensed milk, 1/2 cup cocoa powder, 2 cups heavy cream, 1 cup light cream, 1 Tbsp vanilla extract, 1/2 cup pecans, 1 cup mini marshmallows

Method: my mouth is watering already, and we have not even begun to make it yet. Put a saucepan over a low heat and add in the condensed milk and cocoa powder, cooking it until you have a thickened chocolate syrup, about five minutes would do it. Allow the mixture to cool for fifteen minutes before adding the heavy cream, light cream and vanilla. Place the mixture in the fridge until it is fully chilled.

I am tempted to drink it, but I won't, instead, I am going to chop my pecans into smaller pieces. Pour the chilled mixture into your ice cream maker and press whatever buttons you need to to get it making ice cream. About halfway through (or as instructed by your user manual) add the pecans and marshmallows.

When it is done, eat some of the richest and delicious ice cream ever. Ben & Jerry who?

Peanut Butter Ice Cream Deluxe

Ingredients: 1/4 cup sugar, 3 eggs, cup whole milk, 3/4 cup peanut butter (smooth), 3/4 cup sweetened condensed milk, 1/2 cup half-and-half, 2 tsp vanilla extract, mini peanut butter cups

Method: Grab a bowl and beat the sugar and eggs together until they are thickened and come off your beater in ribbons. Now, take a saucepan and pour the milk into it, place it on a low heat and bring it to a simmer. When you have it simmering, take the pan off the heat and pour the hot milk, slowly, into the egg and sugar mixture, whisking with vigor as you pour.

Once you have incorporated the milk into the egg mix, pour the mix into the saucepan and place it back on a low heat, stirring it constantly as it begins to turn into a custard. When it is thick enough to coat the back of your spoon, remove it from the heat.

Add the peanut butter and whisk it in. Allow the mixture to cool for fifteen minutes and then add the sweetened condensed milk, whacking this too. Next, add the half-and-half (half a cup of half-and-half! Does this make it quarter-and-quarter? I am no good with fractions) and the vanilla. Place the mix in the fridge and allow to cool completely.

Once the mix is cooled, pour it into your ice cream maker and make it do the thing where it takes a liquid and turns it into a solid. As it is doing its thing, take your peanut butter cups (as many as you want) and chop them up. You can make tiny pieces, leave them all whole, or go somewhere in between. When the ice cream is done and still soft, stir in the peanut butter cup pieces. Make sure to go for a 5k run after eating this to burn off the calories.

Extremely Chocolatey Chocolate Ice Cream

Ingredients: 3/4 cups sugar, 1 cup milk, 1/4 tsp salt, 2 Tbsp cocoa powder, 3 egg yolks, 2oz semisweet chocolate, 2 cups heavy cream, 1 tsp vanilla extract

Method: Be prepared to have your mind blown by this super chocolatey ice cream. In a saucepan, over a medium heat, combine the sugar, milk, salt and cocoa powder. Stir the mix constantly until it begins to simmer. As you are doing this, beat the three egg yolks in a bowl. When the mixture on the stove is simmering, pour, slowly about half a cup of it into the egg yolks. As you pour, stir the liquid in. Once it is incorporated, pour the egg mix into the pan and heat until the mixture thickens. Take care not to boil the liquid.

Take off the heat and chop up your semisweet chocolate into small pieces. Stir the chocolate pieces into the mixture and stir until they all melt. Place your mixture in the fridge and allow to cool fully. When it is cool, stir in the cream and vanilla. Pour this into your ice cream maker and allow it to perform its thing. When it is done, you will have chocolate ice cream which will blow all other chocolate ice cream out of the water.

Zingy Lemon Ice Cream

Ingredients: 2 cups heavy cream, 1 cup half-and-half, 1 1/8 cups sugar, 3 Tbsp grated lemon zest, 5 egg yolks, 3/4 cup lemon juice

Method: mix together the heavy cream, half-and-half, sugar and lemon zest and pour into a pan. Place the pan over a low heat and wait for the mixture to simmer. When it does, take it off the heat and cover the pan. Leave it like this for ten minutes.

While those ten minutes are ticking by you can beat the egg yolks in a bowl, and squeeze the lemon juice (if you are not using bottled lemon juice). After ten minutes, place the pan back on a low heat and scoop out a cup of it. Pour the cup of liquid into the yolks, slowly, stirring frequently. Once it is incorporated, pour your egg mix back into the pan. Cook this over a low heat until you get a custard which coats the back of your spoon. It should not take more than ten minutes.

Once you have your custard, transfer it to a bowl and leave it in the fridge overnight. Do not forget to refrigerate your lemon juice too. Once your mix is chilled, stir in the lemon juice and add it to your ice cream maker, using the ice cream maker as you have used it before (unless this is your first time, in which case check the instructions).

Once the ice cream make is finished, freeze the ice cream for a further four hour to give the flavors time to liven in the mix. Serve as a palate cleanser after a heavy meal of roast pork with all the trimmings.

Well, that is the last recipe I am going to give you. Do not look at me like that, I have given you over a hundred recipes, or under a hundred recipes, one of the two. Anyway, that should be enough for you to be getting on with. The only thing to do now is to wrap up this book unless you want to know some of my super-secret ice cream making tips? Check out the next chapter to see if you deserve them.

Ice Cream Making Tips

I was not going to do this, but you have been such an attentive reader that I am going to let you in on my secret tips for making successful ice cream at home. Without further ado, here they are:

- We have talked about ice cream makers and freezing the bowl before adding your mixture. Get in the habit of storing your bowl in the freezer so that you are never caught short.
- Cold ingredients make quicker ice cream. Make the mixture in advance and keep the mixture in the fridge overnight to quicken the process with any ice cream making method.
- With any recipe that calls for egg yolks, if you add hot liquid too quickly to the eggs they will scramble, and that is almost the opposite of ice cream.
- Alcohol can be fun (for adults, definitely not for kids), but more alcohol means more time to freeze, or your ice cream not freezing at all. Use alcohol to flavor, not to booze your ice cream up.
- If you want to mix any additional ingredients into your ice creams, such as chocolate chips or chunks of peanut brittle, add them in right at the end of the process for the best results.
- Shallow containers will help your ice cream to freeze quicker and will make it easier to mix and to scoop.

•Home made ice cream uses fresh ingredients and no preservatives, additives, etc., so you should try and eat it within a week or it will begin to lose flavor

•If you sub ingredients for low-fat alternatives, you will save some calories, but the ice cream will not state as good.

•Have fun when making. Seriously! Ice cream eating is a fun pastime; ice cream making should be the same. Do not be afraid to experiment and try new things. Find out what you like and what you don't like and make some great ice cream.

Well, that is about it for ice cream making. All that is left is to wrap this up with a short conclusion.

Conclusion

Ice cream had some humble beginnings, starting out as flavored ices and developing into the crazy assortment of desserts we all know and love. I wonder what Hippocrates would make of our modern ice cream and whether he would prescribe it to his patients or not. As far as I know, ice cream is not seen as a health food, or is it? No, it most definitely is not. It is yummy though!

Well, what a journey we have been on. We have learned of four ways of making ice cream: the food processor method, the bag method, then freeze and stir, and the ice cream maker. All four methods have easy recipes, and all four are capable of making some delicious ice cream that you can be proud of.

Try out the recipes and see what works for you. Substitute different ingredients, making sure not to lose out on the quality of your finished product. Some of the methods and recipes take no time at all, while some take all the time in the world. In this day and age, it is nice sometimes to slow down and do something right. Do something with care. Put your heart and soul into it.

If you do this right, you will be feeding your heart and soul, as well as the hearts and souls around you. Once you have mastered ice cream making, you will never buy ice cream from a store again. I am not going to tell you that this book will change your life, for once you start making the recipes in this book, you will see that your life is changed.

Good luck on your journey to the land of sweet treats and frozen goodness. Pick up your spoon, thrust it in the air and claim your spot as a hero for the ages. An ice cream make like no other. The king who will be sung about in a son of cream and ice!